DONNA

Sex, Wisdom, and Servitude

MYARASHAD.COM

DEDICATION

To Rebecca, Bertha, Retta and every woman in my
maternal line: I quite literally wouldn't be here without
you. I cherish the lessons you've passed down to me.
Your stories will forever be a part of me.

PROLOGUE
WOMEN

Decolonize your understanding of womanhood, feminism & sex based violence.

Globally there are more than 28 million women and girls who are enslaved. They're raped, beaten, and denied adequate education. Feminism should be about protecting those women and realizing that there are far worse horrors than those that westernized feminists present as standard.

If you're reading this and, like me, are living a life of relative privilege, consider this a call to decolonize your understanding of womanhood and to become a better feminist.

If you are a woman who was born into slavery or extreme oppression: I love you. I cherish you. Your voice is important. You are the feminist that the world needs. You are the future of womanhood. Your pain, sweat, and tears are why women like me can write poetry about sex, wisdom, and servitude.

DONNA

She was a girl without a home, spending her
last days on earth collecting the birthright she
had been deprived of.

Her scars were a permanent reminder of her
minuscule worth; no matter how much effort she
sowed, she wouldn't hide them.

While the village women fought against sexual
persecution, she yearned for the warmth of
a warrior, and the safety of a patriarch.

If God wouldn't bless her, she would soon
use the withered scraps of yesteryear
to bless herself.

ARÉ

We built castles encased in concrete;
we drew bushes surrounded by love,
and nature and everlasting lust.

We tamed a forest of tweed and silk,
and blew past the murky corridors
of insidious disdain.

We fought with the dynamite of our love,
crowning ourselves victors in our celestial fun
house; a calm breeze often mistaken for paradise.

MUSTAFA

Even awake, he dreamt of a world filled with her face;
he was always alert and aware of how his large
frame fit so well between her full hips.

His palette was one of remote meager sensations,
but he had a thirst for the illicit taste of her lips after
her unrivaled devotion; he could die for her love.

She sowed a fortress with his sins and built a home
from his fears. This life of his wouldn't ever be complete
without the sounds she makes upon arrival to ecstasy.

SILO

I dreamt of the
lingering taste of
surrender,
and fell into a
luscious heaven
of his weight,
his scent, and his
desire for me.

AGILE

She showed you
the way to her
hips, and It
became your
pathway to exile;
a journey filled
with sweet
release.

"The only time a Muslim gets real violent is when someone goes to molest his woman. We will kill you for our woman."

—El Hajj Malik El Shabazz, formerly Malcolm X

"The most disrespected person in America is the Black woman. The most unprotected person in America is the Black woman. The most neglected person in America is the Black woman [...] and the only time a Muslim gets real violent is when someone goes to molest his woman. We will kill you for our woman."

—El Hajj Malik El Shabazz, formerly Malcolm X

RAMI

You handle my soul like it's made of glass;
fragile and prone to breaking, its delicate nature
drives your inclination to protect it.

Seeking problems before they become deadly;
eliminating chaos before it reaches my agave-drenched lips;
all so you can be the man God sanctioned you to be.

You are a man that exists outside the confines of
perfection; and for that, you're a better man than
most could ever dream of becoming.

PART ONE

SEX

A man can never know the full extent of the abuse his wife has suffered.

All he knows is the woman she presents herself as, and all he can be is grateful that God gave her the strength to love him, despite her better judgement. Women heal themselves, then go on to turn ordinary men into kings, all while staying silent about their oppression.

SIRE

I've been lonely before;
right when the clock struck seven, and his
fist danced with the sorrow of my chin.

I've been tired too—
but never too tired to sing sweet rhythms,
and whisper sweet nothings as you sleep.

Our withered destiny is amoung us, where
the eve of the pit of my selfishness rides the
wave of your wet crows feet.

The end of my chapter zero was
enough to build skyscrapers; but we've
found ourselves at chapter one.

The silent monuments of my devotion to you
have been demolished with a love that is
only matched by God.

So for now my love, you suffer—
but not for long.

RAHA

He awoke, yearning for the smell of her hair.
He saw himself buried in a cloud of her love,
but to his detriment, he slept alone.

Nothing could prepare him for the view of his
lost lover; the sight of his unreclaimed donna
was illuminating, but reserved for another.

He was enchanted by her golden décolletage;
charmed by her amorous laugh; enthralled by
her brevity; but no amount of newfound
adulation would buy her.

This woman wasn't his ill-forgotten lover,
but his lust persisted; despite her insolent gaze
of fascination, he had a hunger for her; one that
would never be satisfied.

ABDULLAH

The signature of your destiny is one of pain,
but through all of your personal storms,
you find the strength to be a healer.

You're the warrior we never asked for;
a love-starved loner described as
the most righteous soul.

Adorn yourself with the love of God,
and allow the twisted world to weep
at the destruction of your good will.

Don't you dare ever pray for me;
your prayers pierce through me;
forever.

FOREVER

The golden sun shines, and
glides across your beige-brown skin.

You're not a man I'm used to to,
but you're a man that cares—
that, I am used to.

A man that builds the home for his family;
a man that feeds the soul of his wife.

A man that bridges intellectual gaps;
a man that sees the writing on the wall.

The once-colorful sky strikes an overcast,
and you take to bury your sorrowful tears
—but only in the bosom of your God.

GIRL

What is left to say when I'm
at a loss for decadence?

The only words to fall from my
citrus-coated lips are of sweet
disgust and ill-forgotten pain.

She was an innocent child of God,
openly giving from her heart,
so despite our tears,

we must honor her.

HMD

The love of your crows feet
Is the love that I cherish.

Your glistening smile on the
Eightysixth day of eternity is
Like the sweet nectar of God,

Gliding across my lips.

The sweat dripping from the space
Between where our love meets and
The wind blows extends my love
To your deep, salivating eyes.

The might of your soul destroyed
An avalanche of my dark sorrows,
While following the dark, dreary
Mood of my internal drum.

The love is there,
The love is here,

And the stakes are
Brilliantly divine.

Give in to the deepest
Depths of our unsung souls,
Blissfully playing up on the love,

Within you.

PART TWO
WISDOM

For the longest time, I was angry with God—but that was before I knew who he was.

I would sit beside him on long trips through the desert; we would listen to the music of lovers, and while he enjoyed the sounds I sat frozen by the sway of his hands. As his right hand would gravitate towards my inner thighs, I found myself lost in the clouds, praying that the molestation would be enough to temper his ever-changing moods.

I look back at those memories with feelings of great gratitude. I didn't understand my place in the world, but through wisdom, pain, blood and salt, I emerged a new woman.

DUSA

He beat me until I could taste the blood of our ancestors.
A good boy gone rogue, he was as cruel and
venomous as the one before him.

The love that he desired was a love I couldn't give
—so I became a slave to him; an object to be
bought, sold, and distributed as he saw fit.

My bruises were black, and colorless, and
imperceptible to the ears of justice; as I sought
peace, I found myself in siloed defeat.

AMAL

If he loved you
he would
bring the
moon to your
doorstep,
and never
miss a breath.

Darkness
overcame her
bloodshot
eyes—and her
wounded soul
began to
bleed.

OPEN

REIGN

We felt the breeze of the western coastline,
and built a modest safe haven in the face of chaos
—and just as the stars in your eyes dimmed,
I found myself fearing death.

I loved you until my tears ran bloody;
my love lingered until I could taste your sins.

I fought for the beauty of your mind, and
chased the fire of your soul; I bled, I fractured,
I scarred, and somehow I found a pathway to heaven.

BILAL

His teeth grind themselves ragged
replaying the gruesome scenes
of a woman he once loved.

The chaos that builds in his mind
only satiates the wounded, the
heartless and the hungry.

The screams of his inner child
can only be heard by women
looking for a feast.

SKIN

I don't hate the skin of my people,
I hate the hope that trickles down
my smiling face as I inhale.

The strength of your discord
has revealed all that I have
been deprived of.

The toughness of your skin Is
enough to make my scars
visible to the naked eye.

The blood I've lost will forever
stain the hue of our blissfully
sanctioned union of love.

FEEL

I keep the core of
my love soft, and
plush; the window
of my unrivaled
devotion opens
to a scene of you
lost in your own
mirage.

It doesn't hurt
when you arrive;
as our oral
transgressions
fall onto deaf ears,
we find ourselves
unraveling
a storm.

PULL

PART THREE

SERVITUDE

The sex between a man and his wife is sacred when acted upon with mind-fulness of God.

There are no secrets, no hidden desires, no struggle and no attitude; just two people coming together, and stepping into a new world of lust and unknown gardens of ecstasy.

MOHAMMAD

He stood behind my half-naked body in front of our bathroom mirror, placing one hand on my stomach while gently rubbing and cupping my breasts with the other.

"Is this OK?" he quietly whispered.

"Yes."

He began kissing my neck and shoulder.

"Do you want to make love? Tell me the truth."

_____

It had been exactly two weeks following our wedding day, and I was nervous. I've had sex before—I've been married before; but this time was different.

I failed in my first marriage. I married to be loved rather than to give love; to feel secure, rather than to provide security—and when the dust settled, I was left with nothing more than a broken heart and a fractured ribcage.

I struggled to find my worth, and just as I began to slowly heal and center myself, I met Mohammad.

His smile was as gregarious as his loud, billowy laugh. His eyes were dark, deeply set and decorated with the crows feet of a young 30-something.

He made me smile; he prioritized me. He made me feel safe, cherished, and loved. Anything I needed, anything I desired, he would oblige. No request was ever too unreasonable; no gift too grand.

I remember our first conversation about sex. We had been dating for a little over a month, and I told him that I was celibate, and didn't plan on having sex with anyone other than my next husband.

He smirked and joked innocently, "So you've only had sex with one man?"

I sighed and cautiously began to unload my baggage. "Make that two" I said, anticipating his response, "I was also raped."

After a few moments of intensity he wrapped his arms around my waist, and pulled me into his chest. "I should not have said that. Forgive me."

We sat like that for an hour; me, breathing deeply onto his neck; him, gently rocking me back and forth while trying to hide the silent tears coming from his eyes.

Every time we speak about sex, it is always as intense, loving, and honest as that first conversation; but this night will be different because we won't be talking about sex, we will be enjoying it.

DON

The marks he leaves on my body are as dark as his deep, smoldering eyes. As he begins biting, and sucking, and clawing his way to love, I find myself lost in ecstasy.

Even on the days we transgress through to forbidden love making, he always delays the final act.

I become entangled in a web of lust and faint cries for mercy and punishment. Kissing his chest is only the start of my paradise.

"Take me in, and I will be gentle," he says with eyes filled with deep devotion, "deny me and I will rip through you."

Surrender has never been so just, so loving, so divine, so not-understood.

SIN
SYRUP

We've waited all day for this. The kids are
asleep, and the moon is as clear as
the sky is navy.

I'll never get enough of you.

We are bonded by sin and syrup and
anguish and love and light.

Our union is heavenly; blessed by God;
our home is a warm ground zero; a re-
constructed safe space for the fallen angels
of dogma, where we rejoice in the reunion
of our father and his withered children.

The pressure of you entering my yearning
womb elicits my primal sensibilities. The
more we make love, the more our children
see that love isn't something to be bought,
sold, or given freely.

DONNA NEGRA

His lips curled as he awoke from his slumber.

The long, whispy beard hairs that I loved so much gently brushed against my forehead for a good morning kiss that made me feel like a princess.

To most, he was an average-looking man; to me, he was nothing less than a king.

His dark features accentuate his beige-brown skin.

"It's funny, you call my people brown, but I am just barely brown," he says with a smirk.

He always smiles when I use political euphemisms. My heart of gold is a perfect match to his divine intellect.

He makes loving my enemies palatable, and meets my righteous indignation with care and love and submission only shared with God himself.

He doesn't submit to God in my name, he surrenders to me in God's name.

He blesses me when I slumber; prays over me when we feast. He's my father, my lover, the masculine ear of our home.

The darkness of his eyes makes my knees weak. The strength of his character makes me salivate. His long arms, blackened by endless rows of hair seduce my lips apart while the certainty in his voice relaxes my jaw. The firmness of his grip reminds me of the gentleness of his stroke—steady, not hard; deep, not rough.

When we make love, I become a new woman. When I exhale wrath and anger and chaos, he inhales—then breathes new life into me.

My body isn't afraid of him; his aura is a welcome guest inside of my womb.

THE
HELM
OF
SILK

He stood behind me, staring deeply in the reflection of my eyes.

He kissed my neck and gently massaged my empty womb. "I want our children to look like you; your skin, your hair, your eyes; dark, beautiful, pure."

He buried his face in my neck and moaned the name of God.

"Bring us peace," he cried.

www.ingramcontent.com/pod-product-compliance
Lightning Source LLC
LaVergne TN
LVHW010022070426
835508LV00001B/13